14 COLLECTED INTERMEDIATE QUINTETS

THE CANADIAN BRASS

HAL•LEONARD®

GAVOTTE
from Suite for Unaccompanied Violoncello No. 6 in D Major, BWV 1012

Horn in F

Arranged by Henry Charles Smith

Johann Sebastian Bach
(1685-1750)

PRAYER
(Abendsegen)
from *Hänsel und Gretel*

Horn in F

Arranged by Henry Charles Smith

Engelbert Humperdinck
(1854-1921)

CANTATE DOMINO

from *Musica Divina*

Horn in F

Arranged by Henry Charles Smith

Giuseppe Ottavio Pitoni
(1657-1743)

*Play the piece twice through; no ritard. nor fermata the first time.

THE LIBERTY BELL

Horn in F

Arranged by Henry Charles Smith

John Philip Sousa
(1854-1932)

THE DRUNKEN SAILOR

Horn in F

Arranged by Terry Vosbein

Traditional

GREENSLEEVES

Horn in F

Arranged by Terry Vosbein

Traditional

HAVA NAGILA

Horn in F

Arranged by Walter Barnes

Traditional

HIGH BARBARY

Horn in F

Arranged by Terry Vosbein

Traditional

JUST A CLOSER WALK

Horn in F

Arranged by Don Gillis
Adapted by Walter Barnes

Traditional

LONDONDERRY AIR

Horn in F

Arranged by Terry Vosbein

Traditional

SHENANDOAH

Horn in F

Arranged by Terry Vosbein

Traditional

SIMPLE GIFTS

Horn in F

Arranged by Terry Vosbein

Traditional

THIS AND THAT
(Questo e quella)
from *Rigoletto*

Horn in F

Arranged by Henry Charles Smith

Giuseppe Verdi
(1813-1901)

PILGRIM'S CHORUS
from *Tannhäuser und der Sängerkrieg auf Wartburg*

Arranged by Henry Charles Smith

Richard Wagner
(1813-1883)

Horn in F

THE CANADIAN BRASS

CONTENTS

SCORE AND PARTS AVAILABLE SEPARATELY:

Conductor's Score	50486959
Trumpet 1 in B-flat	50486954
Trumpet 2 in B-flat	50486955
Trombone	50486957
Tuba	50486958

ALSO AVAILABLE IN THIS SERIES:

17 Collected Easy Quintets	50486953

U.S. $12.99

HAL•LEONARD®
CORPORATION

7777 W. BLUEMOUND RD. P.O. BOX 13819 MILWAUKEE, WI 53213

www.canbrass.com
www.halleonard.com

ISBN 978-1-4234-8423-3

HL50486956